Memories
OF A MISGUIDED
ROSE

Journey of Love, Heartbreak and Self Discovery

Rosena M. Duncanson

© 2022 Rosena Duncanson

All rights reserved.

No part of this publication may be reproduced, stored in a retrieval system, or transmitted, in any form or by any means, electronic, mechanical, photocopying, recording, or otherwise, without the written permission of the author.

Published by Distinction Publishing House
Dover, Denver, Colorado
United States of America
www.distinctionpublishinghouse.cm

ISBN: 978-1-7374023-3-6

This book is printed on acid-free paper.

Printed in the United States of America

Table Of Contents

Dedication 7

Out of Love 8

Losing Pieces 9

Empty 10

Let Me Know 11

Not Ready To Let Go 12

The Pain of Truth 13

Promises 14

Just Ask 15

You Matter That Much 16

In the Dark 17

Silent Treatment 18

Broken Pieces 19

Senseless Cries 20

Women's World 21

The Noise of Silence 22

The Present 23

It's Really All About Me 24

Love Residue 25

Complex 26

The End 27

Enemy 28

TO BE LOVED 29

Baby Mama Drama 30
The Man of My Dreams 31
Release 32
Connection 33
One Week 34
Erotic Thoughts 35
Limitless 36
Our World 37
Into His Eyes 38
Friend Zone 39
Struggles of Love 40
Thoughts on Valentine's 41
Speak to Me 42
Wonder 43
Moving Forward 44
My World 45
Purpose Filled 46
Hard Love 47
Losing Control 48
Cost of Love 49
When is Enough, Enough? 50
If 51
Little Ones Cry 52
Lifetime Choices 53
Beyond Love 54

Perception 55
Reminiscing 56
Life 57
More 58

True Love 59
Hope 60
Serenity in Chaos 61
More Than Enough 62
For You 63
My Dear Friend 64
I Stand Alone 65
You Are Loved 66
Be Encouraged 67
Mirror 68
Surprises 69
Possibilities 70
Passing of Time 71
Closure 72
What Makes Her Better Than Me? 73
Strength 74
Peace on Earth 75
Evolution 76
Peace 77
Self-Reflection 78
Rebirth 79
Silver Lining 80

Growth 81

Soon 82

Seeds of Life 83

Secrets 84

Trust 85

Dedication

This book is dedicated to the people who have stuck by me through it all - love, heartbreak, and self-discovery.

To my mom, dad, sister, and brother, who have tolerated the laughs, the smiles, the cries, and the mood swings and loved me despite it all,
I say thank you and I love you.

OUT OF LOVE

Losing Pieces

I thought you were the one
To end this vicious cycle of love, lust and lies
Nights of tears, confusion, mistakes, heartaches

Another piece is lost
A piece of my heart

The next must bring a piece with him
When he leaves, he can take it back with him
What else will be left to keep my heart beating,
If this doesn't stop?

Empty

Reaching for something that does not exist
Dreams that never seem to come true

Hallucination - you think it's there, but it is not
Not how you need it to be

Space - so much there is a void
Like a black hole
Empty - a feeling without you

Let Me Know

Reassurance, confirmation, explanation
Though actions speak louder than words
Sometimes words are all that seem to be understood

So tell me what I need to know
So I can decide which way to go
What should I do, stay or leave

Things can be interpreted in so many ways
Ruining many hearts and many lives
So, to avoid me having the same downfall
Simply let me know

Not Ready To Let Go

I say I love you
I show you with my ways
You know I love you
You seem to use it against me

I don't want to lose
Don't want to see you hurt
I only want what's best

I have feelings too
Even though I care about you
I can't kill myself just because you ask me to

Don't need a knife, gun, bridge or a rope
To choke me with
The type of pain my heart will face
I might just be better off dead

Sacrifice, a word once used
I will do for you, if you don't make me choose
Sacrifice, no cable, no phone

I'm not asking to be left alone
Just let me nurture, just let me grow
Let me do the things
I'll do better than you know

I don't want it to be over
I don't want you gone
I want you, me, and this beautiful blessing from God

The Pain of Truth

It makes me cry
Knowing I can't share what I feel inside
The time is not right, but is it ever?
The truth hurts me more than it will ever hurt you
Like a bomb just waiting to explode
Can't be avoided

Promises

Promises are clouds
Changing with the weather
Moving with the wind

Difficult to hold down and collect
Just about impossible; sometimes unobtainable
When you least expect it, they change
To give a very disappointing experience

It's like the saying goes
A promise is a comfort to a certain class of people
How can someone promise you the world?
When even the end of it is unknown

Just Ask

You cut me just to see if I bleed
Push, taunt, and tease
Beg and plead for me to give in, but I don't
Surprise that I am similar, but different
Not different, but similar

I cry and I feel
Have a need to be pleased
But there is more to make this clock tick
Than a twist and a turn

Something special, but unrevealed
Almost magical if you believe
My blood runs red
Just ask, I would've told you

You Matter That Much

You made me feel like I did wrong
Like my actions just weren't right
The song "Silence" God knows I hate the tune
Emotions not said, feelings not shared
The words couldn't be heard

A short answer is just as bad
Like a sentence is more energy than you can muster
A simple phrase, some word cluster
I thought we were growing,
Communication included a give and take type thing

I'll never know how you feel inside
If you never say a thing
Things that bother me won't be used to my advantage
Just know to be cautious next time
The last thing I want to bring is hurt

You matter that much to me
Because of the words that were not said,
the feelings not shared
I am going to cry myself to sleep
Leaving today as a mere memory
Hoping when I wake the pain will go away

In the Dark

You let me fall, your hand I let go
Rock bottom I didn't hit, but humbleness I found
You touch my heart, happiness is lost

I opened every door, not one seemed right
The one I let close behind me
Was where I left you behind
Like walking backwards with my eyes close
How could I feel any more lost?

Silent Treatment

You did me wrong and I should hate you
I shouldn't even want to talk to you
But I would rather be the one to make that call

The decision that we shouldn't talk
Should be something that I control
Maybe it's my mind or more my nerves
I just like to be in charge

From this day on I'll just be me
The silent treatment will come from me
I run my life; it's up to me
I will give the silence back to him
What goes around comes around

Broken Pieces

When you found me, I was broken
Pieces everywhere, my life was in shambles
No one seemed to care

Generosity you showed me
You tried to pick me up
Piece by piece you tried to put the pieces where they fit

Not too much time has passed
Mending isn't complete
You want us to have a future
But you say something is missing

I try to show all I can
That I am doing all I know
You keep insisting that maybe I should leave

You say that I don't know what I want
You say that I'm confused
Maybe the piece I am missing could just be you

Some time it will take to see where you fit
So I can have it all together
If you feel the wait is too long,
Then maybe you need to do what's best

I don't want to lose a special friend
Someone who helped me heal
But I don't want a rerun of a "Broken" episode

With my feelings and my heart
Allow yours to do what's best
Because it's only human nature
For us to protect ourselves

Senseless Cries

I hear you whisper amid the darkness
Words I choose not to hear.
I let the voices in my mind start a cry,
A cry, a cause unknown.

Women's World

She waited, watched,
Listened and learned.
Things didn't go her way.

He was selfish, concerned with himself,
His emotions, feelings, wants, and desires.

Availability was all he wanted,
No commitment, nothing permanent.
Just there, be there waiting, watching,
Listening and learning.

He didn't need to wait, watch, listen or learn.
His mind was made and so was he,
Selfish; leaving her to wait, watch, listen
And learn the ways of a man.

The Noise of Silence

How loud silence speaks,
Echoing with anger in our head
When something is wrong or doesn't go our way.

Silence, filled with tension, anxiousness,
Making blood boil
Flowing at high speeds through our bodies.

Silence that increases our heart rates,
Heartbeats never heard before
Boom...Boom...When there's silence.

Silence, those words unspoken
That could have kept the peace.

Silence, stirring up anger, discomfort bad feelings,
From those unsaid emotions, thoughts.
The noise, the unheard noise within us,
In our heads under our skin.

The noise of silence can bring back memories -
Memories of laughter, cheerfulness, time well spent,
The giggles from playful acts,
The moans and groans,
Silence.

The Present

No one really lets go of the things in our life.
It's not as simple as a string.

There are no ends that can be cut off
To give you new beginnings.

It's not easy to forget
We have no eraser for the mind.

The thing we can thank time for,
Is giving us reason to move on.

There is no chance of turning back,
Just making use of the present.

Only time will let you know
How you will make out with tomorrow.

It's Really All About Me

It didn't matter.
They were empty words.
Words without meaning.

That's all he heard from the words she said.

His mind was made.
He had been hurt and she wasn't right.
She's a woman emotional, unbalanced, and unsure.

Only his feelings matter right?

Love Residue

Here we go again.
You think by now she would be over him,
With her new life and her new friends.
Emotions spent thinking she would marry him.
You think she would forget and try to move on.

It's not like he cares about her.
He has his life and all her friends.
That's maybe why she must hear his name.

Could it all just go away; a bad dream,
To wake up and face reality.
But she can't wake up because she's not asleep.
What she sees now is reality.

A beautiful life with new friends,
Willing to help her out even hold her hand.
Memories don't fade but they can be replaced.

Life is so golden.
The past filled with mistakes and misery.
To be corrected with each step,
To reach perfection.

Complex

Trust and obey
It's too easy to do
Life just has to be complicated,
Challenging, dangerous, suspenseful
Or it just would not be fun.

The End

Who would have thought?
It would ever come to this.
All this time, we still don't have friendship.

A product of time and no communication,
It's too bad we couldn't let conversation flow.

You want to spend time and play with my mind
Leaving me with no clue of who you are inside.

I'm going to move on.
Unless you are willing to change.
To tell you the truth, I'm tired of playing games.

Enemy

The forgiveness thing I've tried
It didn't erase the many nights I've cried
You say you want to be my friend
With the silence, our friendship came to an end

You showed how much you cared
Said you'd always be there
You proved you could lie
With sincerity in your eyes

Questions arise, how I can fall
Then you act like nothing ever went wrong
You took away my joy
Almost as quickly as I've received it

With the daily passing of life
I'm constantly reminded
I try so hard to forget; make peace
Act like we're cool

At the end of the day, I will look like the fool
You used my heart as a front doormat
Now I have to take it back
Share love with one who will give love back
That someone just is not you

TO BE LOVED

Baby Mama Drama

I'm in love with their father
He's in love with me
He's a part of their life
A beautiful package sent to me

Not trying to be mommy
Just giving them love
Just like family

Don't want to cause no problems
Don't know you to cause pain
Because of your title, I could never ask you to go away

From a woman to a woman
A title given to adults
Realize you had your chance with him
Right now your luck is out

I'm not asking to be friends
Not even asking you to be nice
Realize this arrangement
Is something we can't avoid
Avoid the drama, avoid the pain
No need to point, what's done is done
Let's all move on
Show the kids what love's all about

The Man of My Dreams

A part of me grafted like a limb to a tree
A new fruit different, unique
Only a possibility of this creativity

Love, a word I say to you
Feeling felt for you
The outcome of us being one

Forever, a lifetime and a day
Maximum amount of time I want to share with you
The minimum, no less than forever

A day, 24 hours less the time I am asleep
But then, I'm dreaming about you
Wishing you were here sharing my space

A day, the time we will take
One day at a time to complete this race

Faith, hope, love,
The power of prayer
All we need for you to remain near

A comfort, a friend
The only one true
The man of my dreams
Is that person you?

Release

You have touched me in ways
I have never been touched before
The warm caress, gentleness
Not physical
Emotional, sensual, mystical, amazing
You appeared to set me free

Connection

He is my King, I am Empress Divine
Being with him makes my whole body smile
Nothing 'bout' sex, it 'ain't' that type of feeling
Not some one-night stand or little cheap fling

This thing we share is for real
It's all about him and all about me
Not contaminated with my body
But all about my mind, my heart
How I really feel inside

He makes me feel so special, just like a Queen
I'm addicted to his touch, his presence, his smile
I just have to be with him all the time

I don't want to be a pest
So he doesn't know how much I miss him
But it just feels so good whenever I am with him

Two different people with similar pasts
Although he has more years of experience
We meet at the same level
When they say opposites attract
They are talking 'bout' - me and him
Believe it or not, from day one we have been friends

The greatest love some can ever find
Is in a true and honest friend
In royalty we will continue to grow
King and Empress Divine

One Week

Heaven watch over my friend
While I am away from him
Him from me
Though it is only a week
It is going to feel like an eternity
From day one to seven literally
168 hours give or take a few.

Heaven keep him safe
While he is away from me
Heaven help him
When he gets back to me
Remind him he is always on my mind
From day one to seven literally.

Erotic Thoughts

Your kiss, how I have longed for it
Days felt like weeks, months, years
For that electric touch so passionate

A feeling so erotic
A world I am placed in
When my lips touch yours
High and above the reach of any other

Nothing else seems to exist
Time actually stops
Nothing else matters
When my lips touch yours

A feeling indescribable
Yet I try to anyway
Though unexplainable
But I want it to happen anyway
To float away with you

In a world untouchable by the hands of time
My body smiles
With a pleasure unsurmised
Just because your lips touched mine

Limitless

Some mountain tops seem unreachable
Like a goal unobtainable
A task that just cannot be completed
Not enough time

This feeling that I feel for you
Unlike a mountain, goal, or task to do
Is limitless to the hands of time

Can't call it love
And lust is too harsh
And infatuation is far past gone

We will talk right now and talk some more
Some time will pass and then some more
I will fall, you will fall and get back up
Or maybe not

Lost like the seconds on the clock of yesterday
The moments that will never see tomorrow
Unless you are willing to continue holding my hand

Our World

A precious pearl amongst the rocks of the world
I found you hiding in the shell you call home
You allowed me to move you
Make you my own.

I am your pearl, and you are my own
We'll have to create a new shell

Call it our world.

Into His Eyes

She looked into his eyes and saw reflections of herself.
She saw what she looked like through his eyes
A mere reflection like a mirror, superficial, an insufficient view.
She had to look deeper if she wanted to know more.

She looked into his eyes and saw memories of yesterday.
She saw emotions in his eyes, unfinished business,
And unfinished conversations.
Eyes that spoke a thousand languages, all understood
By the one who dared time enough to look; but there was more.

She looked into his eyes and saw the past, beyond yesterday.
The past covered with dust from years of not being touched.
She saw those relationships gone bad
That kept him from moving on.
She saw the relationships that were good
That made a relationship worth being in.
She saw some things locked
And marked never to be opened again.

She looked into his eyes, like her, there was a past, present
And future; touched, untouched, and soon to be created.
She realized he too had secrets and experiences
That had an impact on his character, personality, and attitude.

She learnt patience and understanding.
She looked into his eyes and wanted him to see her
As she was trying to see him as different, but similar.

She looked into his eyes looking for the future
That soon to be a mystery
Her part in the present is her key to the future.
Look but don't touch is a statement to a child.

Friend Zone

Words can't describe the true feelings of one's heart.
I know that you care
I hope you know I care for you.

Friendship is the beginning
Love is somewhere near the end.
In time I hope we may meet somewhere in between.

Struggles of Love

I feel my heart racing and my body getting warm.
It feels so good when he holds me in his arms.
Too bad that's not all there is to these relationships.
Sometimes it feels like a chore,
Just trying to make it work.

We argue one day and make up the next.
Sometimes I wonder, if it is really worth it?
All the pain I feel inside, the many nights I've cried.
But I love him, is that reason to let your heart die?

People need time to grow,
It's important to let them know,
Exactly how you really feel, you have to keep it real.
Time will tell, but only you will know,
If it's really love!

Thoughts on Valentine's

Love, that mystical, magical word
Filled with pain, happiness, and confusion.

The word used for girlfriend, boyfriend,
Husband, wife, sister, and brother,
No wonder it can get confusing.

A word so short with so much meaning,
You think one day
It would bring about worldwide healing.

Too bad
We only designate one day to really show it.
Happy Valentine's Day.

Speak to Me

I need you to speak to me!
Speak to my body
With your kiss so electric.
Speak to my mind,
With your words filled with intellect.
Speak to my heart
Making me fall in love with you
Over and over and over again.

Wonder

Sometimes we try to figure out why
Why today is different from any other day.
Why we are together and try to stay this way.

What a great probability 50-50
Is it 70-30 or even 40-60?
Does it matter?
Somebody has to bend.

Bend far enough not to break
To pick up the slack
The slack,
The weight of the one being lazy
That day takes two.

If a person wanted to be alone, eat alone, live alone,
Don't you think they would stay alone?
Two great minds with different intentions!
How great are the possibilities of many conflicts?
Aren't there solutions?

To every question, there is an answer.
Never one, at least not all the time.
Remember we have great minds,
Too great to share?

Moving Forward

You have been loved before
Did not take the opportunity to love back
People have cared for you
But you never really cared.

This time it's different.
You love and you care; put yourself out there.
You have been appreciated, but never realized it.
Do you now?

You say what you are used to, how things use to be.
At this time is anything how it used to be.
Can we leave yesterday alone?

My World

My world, would you be willing to share, my world,
It's big enough for two.
Half for me and half for you
We could meet at the equator.
You know somewhere near the center.

I don't want to cry.
Tears of joy are cool, but tears of pain have no gain.
So let me know if this new arrangement; you know me and you,
Is it what you are looking for?
Or would you prefer things how it use to be?
Before I met you and you met me.

Purpose Filled

All she wants to do is sit and cry.
There are no words that can be said
In those moments her tears are shed.

With each drop that starts to fall
There is a story that caused it all.
A story filled with pain and hurt, lies and deceit,
From people considered family.

Each tear that falls is purpose-filled
To free her mind and instill some peace.

Hard Love

Why do we hurt the ones we love;
The ones who loved us first.
For simple flings or some new love
Doesn't family come first?

Why do we hurt the ones we love
With no attention and disrespect.
To prove our individuality;
Show we are different from the rest.

Why do we hurt the ones we love;
Because it seems they hurt us first.
They say two wrongs don't make a right.
Maybe that is what's best.

Why do we hurt the ones we love?
Maybe it's not love!

Losing Control

It's hard to believe, but you control how you feel
You control what you hear and what you see as real

You control how you let one situation control the others
You control, your smile and tears
Unless you are related to me of course

As of late, the control is strained
The happiness you felt seemed to be drifting away
And deep in a shell is where you want to remain

You are my King and I'm your Queen
This relationship we share should be our shield
Block the hurt, the lies, everything else

Cost of Love

Got a rose the other day
Luscious red petals and a green stem
I know one day it was going to die
So, I turned it upside down
With hopes it would dry

Wouldn't be as vibrant
But it would still be mine
Hung it up high so nothing could reach it
But it fell today and lost some of its petals
No matter how hard the effort they wouldn't be returned

Some petals are still there
The rose still exists
Once the other petals disappear
Its role as a rose will be dismissed

When is Enough, Enough?

What do you say to someone
Who doesn't want to hear
The truth because they don't care?

They don't care, because they don't know;
Don't want to know.
Someone sacrificed.
Someone wants the best for them.

What's best may not seem best to you.
They are just trying to keep you under lock and key.
Protect you from the things you cannot see.

You feel they don't care,
Just trying to keep you there.
Keep you where they can see you
Like you are some baby.
But you are, were, and will always be someone's child.

A roof over your head, some sense in your brain.
Life is a two-way street it goes both ways.
The older you get the harder it seems.

Life is a lesson.
When you are tired of learning, I guess you are dead.
Your life is yours and no one else's.
You have matured
When you have learned to handle yours.
Running is not maturing - it's just the punk way out.

If

If we had all the answers how dull life would be.
There would be no expectations and no mysteries.

If we knew the reasons for a mood or unforeseen emotion,
There would be no need for friends
No advisement for problems.

Little Ones Cry

I find it hard to sacrifice
When it's already been done
God's son was the ultimate one
Why does a baby have to die so another can live?
Some doctor, lawyer, or miracle worker
Won't get their chance in the world

Reasons seem valid and intentions seem good
But if they could speak
What do you think they would say?
"Give me a chance I promise to be good"

"Please don't, I just want to live
I won't get in the way; I just want to be loved
You'll be so happy to have me around"

That small little heartbeat at just six weeks
Crawled up in a corner
Wishing it could speak so it could defend itself
Something mommy couldn't do

Lifetime Choices

I've been fighting with myself
This war I know I'll lose
Hardest problem is I can't believe I have to choose
Both decisions are for a lifetime
But one means much more
The beautiful relationship
Between mother and firstborn

Beyond Love

Communication is the door to someone's mind,
The release of the tension;
The answers to the questions why.

What's the use of being together if there is nothing;
not even conversation.
If I didn't want to talk; I'll be better by myself.

Perception

Understanding or selfish; which one should I be
The question playing in my mind
As I venture through life's mysteries
I don't want to seem like a pain
Or somebody's mat
I want to be appreciated
I want to get the respect right back

Understanding or selfish of which has greater gain
Which one will cause the one I love,
A far lesser pain?

Understanding or selfish, the question of the day
Selfish seems to get all the attention,
Understanding sees another day.

Reminiscing

Why can't memories stay buried deep inside?
Just the bad ones that make you cry.
Stay locked away so no one knows.
The ones that just happened to make you strong
Past experience now you stand tall.

Life

Most see it as seclusion, lonely, antisocial,
Total separation, instead of preparation.
Preparation for involvement in an ever-changing world.
As time goes so quickly, no room for stopping
It will go on without you.
Creating eternal separation from a world filled with chaos.
Where no one has control of their life unless they are alone
The world changes who people are or what they do.
So, without being like the world,
Creating control over someone.
Making them out of control
Adding to the never-ending cycle of chaos
Stand alone long enough to gain control of you.

More

This feels so right but can it be so wrong.
Does it depend on how long it goes on or how quickly it ends?
Does it ever have to end or turn into more?
Where we become more than just friends, friends with benefits.

Is it a benefit or just a fun relationship?
Step above friendship less the commitment plus the benefit of
No pain, heartbreak or regret.
Not running the risk of losing this friendship
If this does not work.

As you insist, I will take one step at a time enjoying each
Moment I make you smile.
Watching nature rise and all the benefits of this friendship, fun
Relationship less commitment plus the benefit
Of no pain, heartbreak, or regret.
Not running the risk of losing this friendship
If this does not work.
Until there is more.

TRUE LOVE

Hope

Thank you for making things better
Rainbow after the storm
Dove after the flood
Life after death
You helped me survive

Serenity in Chaos

I feel chained to my past
Working hard to break free
It is those memories that keep haunting me

It is so hard to let go
Erase those memories; good and bad
Trying to emancipate myself
From this "mental slavery" that I have

Though I am happy with how things are
Some things still have to change
Trying to wipe the past away
Giving me a clean slate

Memories keep popping up
Working hard to hold me back
I keep looking straight ahead
The King, my solid rock
The only One consistent
The only One who is right

More Than Enough

A lifetime to complete elevation
We are taking one step at a time
Burning bridges we will no longer cross
Mending ones we know we will face

You and I together, everything will be ok
Living a life of royalty
You are my King and I your Queen
Providing everything in life
Our hearts will ever need

Rich in happiness not with gold
A true love that will never grow old
An open mind realizing differences
An inner peace that calms the storm

Never knew I could influence you
Like you influence me
Nobody really leading
Following the same beat

Two spirits on one accord
Envy to all who sees
This relationship filled with royalty

For You

You know the way I feel for you.
You know the way I smile for you.
You even know I have cried for you.

It's true that I have found love for you.
The time we shared it's all for you.
Baby communication, we try to do.

We try to talk, and we argue too.
That's what we're supposed to do.
It shows that I care for you.

I'll try to tell you all the truth.
I'll try my best not to hurt you.
I know I don't want to hurt too.

We'll grow in love.
And love to grow.
Affection we'll have to show.

Open hearts and open minds.
It's what we need all the time.
I need to know; I don't read minds.

I'll do for you.
You'll do for me.
I Love You.

My Dear Friend

An open ear that has no limit,
A shoulder that held the head of an eye filled with tears.

The encouraging words of one who knows,
And what is not known digs deep to understand.

Unending patience and soft tone
Same voice with rebuke,
When I've done wrong.

Nonetheless still by my side
My Dear friend.

I Stand Alone

In this lonely world,
Filled with misunderstandings and confusion,
I stand alone.

This world, where they try to understand
But never entirely,
I stand alone.

This world with its smart remarks and logical reasoning
Never seeing the real truth,
I stand alone.

I stand alone but not lonely.
An individual with scattered thoughts,
Oceans of emotions.
I stand alone,
But there is One always by my side.

You Are Loved

Day of Red and White and sharing of love
Is all that Valentine's is really about.
But on this day to my dear friend
Who has given an ear that I have poured on,
That dear shoulder that has always been there
Has been soaked with my many tears
That sweet smile that shows she cares.

With all sincerity, she has told me the truth
Though it might hurt she gave me strength.
Through her comments, she has made me wise,
Told me what I needed and opened my eyes.

So, in this time of Red, White, and sharing of love,
I want to tell my dear friend she is loved.
And I will be there, especially because you care.

Be Encouraged

Some people are precious but overlooked,
Not appreciated for all the time they took.
The time they took to show their love,
To meet your needs when none other would.

Journey on through the years of life;
Learn as you move.
Although it's rough, do not give up;
It's not too hard to do.

Many obstacles will come;
Preventing the voyage smooth.
Encouragement I will give;
That's what friends are for.

Mirror

It's just because you think like me,
You really seem to feel like me.
Emotions make you care like me.

We are friends because you communicate with me.
I really appreciate your time with me.

When times are rough, we'll see them through.
When it seems I don't have time,
Just remember I think about you.

There is a reason when I'm not around you,
For you feeling sad and blue.
I must admit I feel it too.

It's not easy to express yourself.
Afraid of rejection,
Thoughts of the past.

I am a friend to you,
It would be nice if you are my friend too.
Communication, love, and respect
Will get us through this friendship.

Because I care for you
I will worry and I will feel for you.
Don't call it pity and let go of your pride.
You said you are by my side.

Surprises

When life is dreary, sad, and dull
This is when God sends someone.

A friend whose ear will hear complaints
Made by you of all your pains.

The unexpected you must expect
From this friend who is compassionate.

The little things they will surprise
So, you must keep open eyes.

Possibilities

Knowing not what the future holds.
Only this I hope holds true
The beautiful and real friendship
Shared by me and you.

Passing of Time

It's amazing how time flies.
And with the passing of time, things change.
We change our minds, our feelings, and our styles.
Things we once did we don't do anymore.
Not because we don't like doing it
Boredom isn't even part of the cause.

We just stop
It seems like the right thing to do.
People don't mean to hurt you by it
They are just following their hearts.
Only time will determine what's in store for us.

Closure

I'm free
I'm me
Closure came today
The things I knew I heard for sure
Feelings have gone out the door

I can now move on true love to find
My full potential now will shine

This smile you see is freedom felt
The laugh you heard was from the heart
Our time has come and quickly gone

What Makes Her Better Than Me?

Is it her smile, her eyes?
The way she does her hair

The color of her skin,
The way she walks.

Is it her voice, her laugh, her age, her size?
Is it the complexity of her mind?

To each his own you hear some say,
This causes us to go our separate ways.

No matter what your reason may be.
There are no reasons she is better than me.

Strength

Strength, ignoring his words,
His cries of pain.

Not forsaking your feelings
For an unconcerned man.

Peace on Earth

People united not because of race, class, or color
But for the sake of love
We lend a hand to meet the needs of our fellow man

Not just men or women, but children too
They need love just like you
Someone to listen to the good and the bad
Just to say the kind of day they had

Evolution

The mind wonders coming up with ideas.
Ideas based upon old experiences.
Decisions made yesterday seem irrelevant,
Null and void.
Then your mind finds its way home.
Decisions of the past are restored.

Peace

In this still silence
My heart beats, mind and emotions wander
Like a roller coaster up and down, round and round
Then it stops and I settle.

Self-Reflection

Rejection is not hard to accept when you expect it.
Being yourself and getting to know yourself,
Trying to develop yourself.
It's all that matters.

Only one person will find true perfection in you, that's you.
Try to please none other than yourself;
Someone will then be pleased with you.

"Free your mind," think create, analyze, dissect.
See what makes the world turn,
In these, you may find yourself.

Rebirth

The tree blowing speaks to me,
My only friend
Lighting strikes and tears it down,
I feel the pain, I lost my friend.
I see the sprout, the little plant.
Everything's new like my little plant.

Silver Lining

Like a rainbow before a storm
Hiding behind the clouds until it's calm
Bringing a smile to at least one face
If only for one day
Just a reminder that everything will be ok

Growth

Early in the morning birds sing,
Children playing, rise with a smile on my face
No worries, no problems, leaving yesterday in my dreams

Realized things can't be changed all the time
I was able to face my fears today
Looked at the past and smiled
Realized I'm bigger than I gave myself credit for

Elevated to another level
More levels to be reached
"One step at a time"
A phrase that once brought pain
Has now become my strength

I couldn't do it alone
Each day my strength is increased
My independence returns

Soon

My heart aches waiting on forever.
For a happily ever after
The world somehow thinks will never come true.
That's unless you settle for some imitation version of
"I love you."
Like some counterfeit will ever be able to
Stand up to the test of time;
With stains that last on your heart beyond a lifetime.

Soon, patiently wait for the creation;
If that's what's necessary,
As your royal counterpart is transformed behind the scenes
With each passing moment in time.
More dramatic than a pumpkin into a chariot,
A glass slipper to reveal if you're a perfect fit.

Don't force it, rush it, or make-believe it; wait for it.
Soon will be here before you know it.
It's only a matter of time,
When the aches become warm welcoming throbs,
In sync with a heart that's meant to be yours.
Just wait for it.
It's coming soon.

Seeds of Life

It was just a moment,
Directed at one person creating a pain that lasted a lifetime.
The effects, like a virus, spread
Now the question is when it will end.

Sadly, selective forgiveness won't fix it.
If you don't use the antidote of love and forgiveness on everything, the infection of pain will start all over again.

It takes one seed of hate, one seed of envy,
One seed of lack of forgiveness
To create or continue a lifetime of pain.
These seeds could just exceed your lifetime.
Be mindful of the seeds you plant.

Secrets

Blue of the sky wondering where my secrets lie.
Somewhere amongst the clouds, hidden from you up high.
Secrets shared with no other.
Secrets that seem best forgotten.

Blue of the sky.
Why with curiosity you ponder?
Ponder what is best untold.
Kept away so no one knows.

Secrets made to lift one high.
Secrets made for an early retire.
Secrets one might find offending
Secrets that may be demanding

Blue of the sky, leave the secrets, let them lie.
Truth could be found from deep within,
That's where your search should begin.
We call them secrets and won't tell a friend.
Blue, wonder what can help not hurt,
Those secrets you should search.

Trust

We say we've moved closer to God
Because he's the only one who can make a bad situation better.

We say we trust him to correct the path we have been walking
Down all these years.

We ask him to show us a sign that we can love again,
Trust again, just be again,
But when bad times appear
Our trust in God seems to go out the door.

We let fear of the past, fear of the unknown,
All the memories of what once were, make decisions for us.
We border on the line of decisively indecisive.

Our constant prayer should remain,
Let go and let God as he truly directs our path
And gives us the desire of our hearts.

www.ingramcontent.com/pod-product-compliance
Lightning Source LLC
Chambersburg PA
CBHW070323120526
44590CB00017B/2796